THE E.S.C.A.P.E. PLAN

The Formula to Creating a Business and Escaping The 9 to 5 Life for Good

DAMIAN AND TIMEESHA DUNCAN

All rights reserved.

The authors and publisher of this book and the accompanying materials have used their best efforts in preparing this book. The authors and publisher make no representation or warranties with respect to accuracy, applicability, fitness or completeness of the contents of this book. The information contained in this book is for education purposes. Therefore, if you wish to apply the ideas contained in this book, you are taking full responsibility for your actions.

As always the advice of a competent legal, tax, accounting or other professional should be sought. The authors and publisher do not warrant the performance, effectiveness or applicability of any sites listed or linked to in this book. This book is for informative purposes and is not warranted for content, accuracy or any other implied explicit purpose.

Now with that said, dive right in and let's get started!

TABLE OF CONTENTS

Dedication 4

Timeesha's Story 5

Damian's Story 12

Introduction 22

Chapter 1: Eliminate Your Fears 28

Chapter 2: Strategize Your Killer Business Plan 38

Chapter 3: Count Your Coins – How to Financially Prepare to Quit Your Job 45

Chapter 4: Attract and Authentically Connect with Your Tribe 52

Chapter 5: Package Your Genius to Create a Magnetic Brand that Steals the Hearts of Your Clients 59

Chapter 6: Expand Your Network, and Build Your Squad 73

Here Is Your 6 Step Escape Plan Formula 78

Conclusion: So Now What? 79

Meet The Power Couple - Damian and Timeesha 81

DEDICATION

THIS BOOK IS DEDICATED TO OUR PRINCES, JADEN AND JORDAN.

Mommy and Daddy wrote this book for you so that you never have to work for someone else in your lifetime. While we are alive, we will give everything to make sure you are the natural born leaders you were meant to be. We want you to not only lead but continue our legacy to show others how to use their talents to live in the purpose and share their gifts with the world.

Love, Mommy and Daddy

TIMEESHA'S STORY

It was Monday morning. The first Monday in forever that I was actually excited to go to work. No one but Damian and my sister, Debbie, knew what I was getting ready to do. I couldn't dare tell my parents. I knew they would be disappointed and then try to talk me out of it, so they were the last people on the planet that needed to know what was about to go down.

The night before I could hardly sleep. My nerves were bad. The anticipation had my nerves feeling like I was on a never ending roller coaster ride at Six Flags Over Georgia. I was committed to going through with it, but I just didn't know what to expect and my mind wouldn't rest.

Ironically, I woke up that morning feeling like I had 8 hours of sleep instead of the actual 2 I really received. I dropped Jaden off to pre-school as I normally did before bustling through the horrible Atlanta traffic, on my way to work.

I remember blaring my radio so loud that I almost bust the speakers in my car. As I turned onto the street of my job, one of my all-time favorite jams came on my Pandora station, *"It's Over Now"* by the R & B group, 112, and it was like God was giving me the confirmation I needed by means of Q, Mike, Slim, and Daron. I sang in my best Beyoncé voice, in the executive parking lot of The Coca-Cola Headquarters and I didn't care not one bit. I mean what were they going to do? Fire me? Lol... I stayed in my car until that song ended, and then I knew it was time.

I remember the butterflies fluttering in my stomach as the elevator rode up to the 24th floor of the North Avenue Tower executive building. I got there before my manager, so I had a chance to collect my thoughts and get my life together. As I sat there, I thought about all the memories I had there. Some good but the last few were bad. Bad because I was so unhappy.

I had spent 9 years at The Coca-Cola Company, working for C-Level Executives. An opportunity that many people dreamed of having. The Coca-Cola Company is the largest beverage company in the world. To be a young black girl from the Bronx, NY with no college degree, starting in the company as a Temp and then becoming a permanent employee working for The President of the Company was definitely a privilege and an honor. But, don't get it twisted, I had to pay my dues. A lot of people were not happy that I was there, but I didn't care. You see, employees of the Company would work 10 years before they could even walk on those floors, and yet, me (young black girl with no college degree) was coming in from the streets to work with the Top Execs of the Company. But I guess soon they figured I was there to stay or they figured I didn't care so eventually the caddy negativity went away.

After 9 long years, I knew my time there had run its course. I was miserable and was suffering from a severe case of depression. I hated being there because it stumped my creativity. I started a business on the side to fill that void of being a free creative, but all it did was make me want out of the 9 to 5 life even more. I told myself I was going to quit so many times before, but never had enough courage (or money) to finally make the move.

A few years back, when I finally decided I had enough of the 9 to 5 life and had planned to quit, my husband came home and kindly showed me the pink slip he was given, that his assignment as a Banking Consultant, had just ended. We had just moved into our brand new 8-bedroom house with a movie theater in the basement, a 9-foot-deep pool in the backyard on 1 acre of land, and an investment property that the tenants just walked out on, so me quit – yeah I don't think so. We were stretching it with the two incomes we had, living above our means, of course, so now that we only had one income - mine, there was no way I was going to give up that "good job" now.

I felt stuck. And to make matters worse, after a time of searching for work with no results, my husband told me that he wasn't going to look for another job and that HE wanted to pursue entrepreneurship. What?! Both us couldn't pursue entrepreneurship with all the bills we had. I was crushed. But, being the ride or die chick that I am, I stepped up to the task of taking care of us, but inside I was miserable, and I blamed him for the next 5 years of suffering we experienced.

I kept hustling my side gig as an Event Planner, but I wanted more. And more importantly, I wanted my husband to get a job... we were struggling pretty bad. No one knew this of course because all they saw was our fancy house, my Mercedes Benz and his Lexus, our lavish lifestyles and our New York swag taking flight in Atlanta.

In 2010, I became pregnant with our first son, Jaden and that's when it finally hit me, that we had to swallow our pride and get rid of our home because there was no way 3 of us were going to survive comfortably there. I put my business on the back burner for a while, it was barely making me money, and I was just overwhelmed with it all.

We moved to a smaller 3-bedroom townhome, and things were okay for a little while. I was on bedrest from my 5th month of pregnancy, and I got to spend the next 8 months' home. So I was happy. But, then it was time to go back to work. I was miserable once again, and the entrepreneur itch came back. I knew there was more to life than pushing papers, paying bills and dying. So I started my quest to find more, to learn more about running a business.

I decided to change my focus from event planning to coaching because I was so good at it and that passion over powered my passion to entertain.

Things were going smooth and shortly after that I became pregnant with our second son, Jordan. This time I was on bedrest from 6 weeks of pregnancy and didn't return to work for almost a year. So you can imagine when it was finally time to go back, I was sick.

Even though I was home bound, I had a taste of what freedom was, and I wasn't ready to give that up. So when I returned back to work, that's when the countdown began.

In March 2015, I made the decision that September 15, 2015, was going to be the day I quit.

September 15th came and while I was mentally ready, my pockets weren't. I let fear creep in and I made the decision to stay a little while longer, you know until my money was right. I made every excuse why I needed to stay a bit longer and decided November would be a better month. But shortly after that date, I realized, nothing was going to change until I did. My manager and I kept bumping heads. I couldn't keep myself bound to a desk, to a check, to a life I didn't want, and it didn't matter how many additional checks I got, if I didn't put my actions behind my words, I would be stuck forever. So 2 weeks later, I did the unthinkable.

My manager walked in her office, and I whispered to myself, "this is it, it's do or DIE." I wasn't going to wait until the end of the day to do it. "It" needed to be done right at that moment. We were about to have our team meeting, where we talked about all the things the team were going to do for the weeks to come, and I wasn't about to take on a whole bunch of work I had no intention of completing so "it" had to be done... now.

After she put her purse down on her desk, my manager, Lisa, came outside of her office to mine and started running off a list of things she wanted me to tackle for the day, and that's when I kindly interrupted her and said, *"Lisa, I need to talk to you for a second."* She looked puzzled and said, *"Oh ok, is everything ok,"* and I grinned and said, *"Yep, it sure is"*. She walked into her office first and I followed and closed the door. That's when "it" happened. I finally did that thing I had been dreaming about for years but thought it would never happen. I finally quit.

I said, *"So I just want to let you know that I will be leaving the company, and here is my resignation."*

There it was. I did "it". I did the unthinkable.

I Quit.

It was like she saw a ghost. She couldn't believe this was happening, and to be honest, neither could I. We both kinda just looked at each other, she looking perplexed as all get out and me standing proud and strong in my conviction. It was at that moment that I knew this was the first day of the rest of my life. I literally felt like the imaginary shackle I had around my ankle instantly cracked in two pieces and the heavy anchor I was carrying over my shoulder shattered to the ground, and I was free.

The biggest gratification was- I didn't need permission to do it. I freed myself. That in itself was the most gratifying thing I had ever done. It didn't matter what she said next, or what I said next, it was done and I wasn't turning back.

3 weeks after I left my job, I sold a program that made over 5 figures in my business. Something I had never seen at my corporate job, in such a short period of time.

Full-time entrepreneurship hasn't been an easy road, but it's one I never regret taking. I have done more in this year than I have ever done for my business. I have met and worked with so many amazing, influential people, I have had the opportunity to be recognized by national publications and was even offered a TV show deal! None of that would have happened, if I stayed stuck behind that desk, wishing and waiting for the right time.

A year from now, you'll wish you started today.

DAMIAN'S STORY

So let me tell you a little bit about me.

I worked for some of the biggest financial institutions in the world, I have an Executive MBA in Business, Certifications out the Wazoo and a tenure of over 20 years in banking and finance. I have managed multi-billion-dollar hedge funds, I am a bestselling author, motivational speaker, transformational coach, created a successful tax business, and promoted some of the sexiest parties in New York City, traveled the world and even worked alongside the biggest entertainer in the world, Michael Jackson. I have always been known as "Most Likely to Succeed", having been an honor student and star football player all throughout my school years. But when I moved to Atlanta, GA with my soon to be wife, everything changed.

Everything was going great, the love of my life and I had moved to Atlanta to start a new life chasing our dreams and goals. We just moved into an 8 bedroom mini-mansion (that's what they call them in ATL) with a pool in back, we had matching luxury vehicles, she had the Benz and I had the Lexus, she was working for the largest company in Atlanta, The Coca-Cola Company and I was working for the 2nd largest financial company in the world trading billions of dollars on the trading floor. I had a consultant gig that was only supposed to last for 3 months. But those 3 months turned into 3 years. I guess I got pretty comfortable, because when they finally told me my assignment was up and gave me my "pink slip", I was in shock.

We had just moved into our home and added an additional $2300 mortgage along with our astronomical monthly expenses of $8592, so now was not the time to not have a consistent paycheck coming in. So I went on my search for a new job. I never did find that job.

My wife was promoted to Bread Winner, against her will, for the next 2 years. And then the one thing we had been praying for happened. We were pregnant with our first son, Jaden.

This creation of life, sparked something inside of me that I had never felt before. I suddenly realized what my purpose was on this earth and it wasn't being stuck behind a cubicle taking orders all day long and generating billions of dollars of others people's money, that I would never see in my lifetime, there of course.

It was time to share my gift with the world. What my wife didn't know was, while I initially was surprised to be laid off, it was only the timing that sucked. I was excited that this was giving me the opportunity to do what I was called to do which was to build my own Sports Academy for Youth and transform thousands of young lives. But I shelved those thoughts to look for work to feed my family.

At that moment, I became pregnant.

Not physically of course, but figuratively with my "VISION BABY."

But it was such bad timing.

So how do I tell my wife that I want to pursue and birth my vision baby?

"OH HECK NO! You need to get a FREAKING JOB and I MEAN NOW," she told me.

I guess she was waiting for her defining moment to bury me six feet under once and for all. And boy did I seal my fate. She continued with a major barrage of destruction of my vision baby.

"Don't you know we have:

- *2 MORTGAGES*
- *2 CAR NOTES*
- *NEED DIAPERS*
- *WIPES*
- *BABY FORMULA*
- *BABY BOTTLES*
- *A BOTTLE WARMER*
- *BIBS*
- *A CRIB*
- *WIPE WARMER*
- *HUMIDIFIER*

- *BABY FOOD*
- *BABY CLOTHES*
- *CAR SEATS*
- *AND DIDN'T I SAY MORE DIAPERS, BABY FORMULA, MORE DIAPERS "*

And the list went on.

The reality hit me faster than a financial tsunami. *"Take what you can get"* said my now resentful wife. She proceeded to run off a list of places I should go work at:

- UPS
- FedEx
- A Diner to Wait Tables
- A Furniture Store
- Deliver Pizzas
- Walmart
- McDonalds

That hit hard like a ton of bricks. I felt so liberated because I finally knew what I wanted to do with my life and yet I was at one of the lowest points in my life simultaneously. Here it is I had over 20 years of experience working for Fortune 500 companies... to just settle for a minimum wage job.

My ego was destroyed. And not only did she want me to settle but then she demoralized me by reminding me of the obvious, *"How can you not find a job with all of your credentials? You're not trying hard enough. I have a job and I have none of the credentials you have. So there is no reason you should not have one."*

As a result of this verbal attack, I experienced the following SIDE EFFECTS:

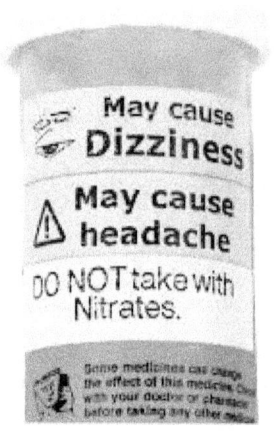

- SELF-DOUBT
- WORTHLESSNESS
- INADEQUACY
- DEPRESSION
- FEELING LIKE A LOSER
- VICTIM of CIRCUMSTANCE
- WALKING ON EGGSHELLS at home
- SELF-HATE
- ME against THE WORLD
- ANGRY

- FED UP
- NOT MATTERING

So consequently, I "aborted my vision baby" and restarted my dreadful job search to appease my "fed up" wife.

Heck, I just wanted her off of my back. So this time, I applied for literally 3500 Jobs over the next 4-year period and I'm serious 3500 jobs (I counted by the way), I only landed 3 Interviews. WOW. Talking about the numbers game not working for me. I was promoted to my new JOB TITLE appointed by my wife: "THE MANWIFE"

We joke about it today. But it sure didn't seem funny back then.

So you are probably saying, "What is a Manwife?" A Manwife is:

- A man that stays home while the wife is the breadwinner
- A man who acts like a wife
- A man who plays the role of a traditional wife (cooks, cleans, takes care of the kids)
- A feminine man in a marriage

You may know this person as: Mister Mom, Mrs. Doubtfire, Daddy Day Care.

Unlike closing Multi-Billion Dollar deals in my past life, My New Job Description was as follows:

- Watch the baby for 9 hours EVERYDAY
- Wash the Dishes
- Go Food Shopping
- Cook Dinner
- Wash Loads of Clothes and Fold Them
- Clean Toilets
- Change "Mudpie" Diapers
- Watch Sesame Street, Maury, Jerry Springer, Family Feud, Dr. Oz, Judge Judy, TMZ, ESPN, The Cat in The Hat, Word Girl, The Depressing News, etc.
- Nurture my child
- Look for Jobs (Remember I had to show my wife I was on the prowl for a job)
- Walk the Dog
- Feed the Dog

- Feed the Cat
- Change the Cat Litter
- Call my friends at work
- Check the negative balance in my Bank Account
- Be secretly ridiculed by Family and Friends "behind my back"
- Request permission to leave the house
- Be called Names such as Daddy Day Care and Mr. Doubtfire

My "career change" was BITTERSWEET."

I was "freed" from Corporate America and Demoted to "Manwife" at the same damn time.

The chitter-chatter from friends and family started to rear its ugly head of how much of an underachiever I became in the eyes of many.

I felt bad because I knew that my wife was miserable at her job and wanted to take her stab at entrepreneurship herself, but she felt stuck and obligated to stay tied to Corporate America because we had mouths to feed.

I tried to encourage my wife to still jump in the water, and pursue her dream of entrepreneurship but at the time it looked like I had two heads. She couldn't see the vision because our reality was looking crazy. But, I knew that together we could take over the world, as a power couple, sharing our God-given talents with the world.

I continued to work on my business as a Motivational Coach and at the same time I took my 20+ years in finance and decided to start my tax business, which gave me a new lease on life. Things were getting better for us both financially and physically.

In 2014, we gave birth to our second son, Jordan.

My wife had been home on bedrest for almost a year due to complications with the pregnancy, so when she finally went back to work, she finally realized this wasn't the life we were supposed to be living, her being chained to a desk and us not living out our purpose.

Then the one thing that I was praying for finally happened.

She came home and told me that she was done and she was putting in her resignation the next day.

I could not have been happier! We had been secretly working on the Quit Your 9 to 5 Academy behind the scenes but for her, it felt inauthentic because she was still stuck at a day job... *"How could I teach someone how to quit their job, when I haven't even quit yet?"*

So she did it. And "WE" birth The Quit Your 9 to 5 Academy.

Since that amazing day, she and I, together have worked with thousands of hustling entrepreneurs to help them transform their lives. THIS IS OUR CALLING.

We are now financially evenly yoked walking in our purpose and we are going to teach you exactly how to do the same thing in this book.

INTRODUCTION

You can't stand Mondays.

In fact, the anxiety of Monday starts Sunday night. The thought of having to go to this godforsaken place another week makes you sick to your stomach.

You hate every single thing about your job, from the annoying micro-manager you have, to the non-fulfilling work you do every single day that a 3-year-old could probably get bored with.

On the flip side you've got a passion to do something more. You've even taken a stab at making it your side business but would love more than anything to do this thing full-time.

You've had enough of this mundane lifestyle but there's one thing...

You don't have any money saved, no real plan that will stick and your business isn't bringing in the type of money you hoped for hence you have an expensive hobby.

So you feel stuck and you're suffocating in the process. You need a way out, a real live escape plan.

Well, you've definitely come to the right place!

Our program The Quit Your 9 to5 Academy and this book was created for creative entrepreneurs who have full-time jobs and hate living the double life of having a boss and trying to be your own boss.

If you are finally ready to take the step from being bossed by someone else to being the boss of your own empire full-time, we are going to show you how to create your perfect escape plan to finally quit your day job you hate oh so much and do what you were called to do full-time.

We know how scary it can be to give up the stability of a steady income every month. That fear of not knowing whether or not you will be able to pay your bills, keep your house, your car, feed your kids, and live the lifestyle you want is a terrible thing.

But the reality is you are doing more harm than good by subjecting yourself to live a life that suffocates you.

You and I both know there is more to life than what you are currently doing right now.

I bet you can see the success of your business and even taste it.

You probably daydream about it all the time but your business aka "your hobby" is not making enough money to allow you to feel confident to quit.

If you are tired of connecting the dots yourself, this escape plan book was created to help you get the most important steps in place so you can finally quit your job and create a successful business with confidence!

NOW FOR THE UGLY TRUTH

Most people think they want to be entrepreneurs because they like what it represents: power, freedom, self-expression, being in control of their life and having authority.

But entrepreneurship requires hard work and dedication.

In fact, if you truly want to have a successful business it takes a whole heap of dedication, discipline, patience, humility, hustle, knee grease (forget elbow grease), sleepless nights and let's throw some blood, sweat, and tears for good measure.

There is no such thing as 9-5, or 40 hours a week.

Your social life will be non-existent in the beginning.

You are your business. If you don't work hard, you don't make money.

Period point blank.

And if you are not about that life, you might as well stop reading this book right now.

I'm not saying this to deter you from being an entrepreneur, but I need you to understand what's at stake. Entrepreneurship is a lifestyle so once you quit your job there is no turning back, so we want to make sure you are in it for the long haul. Not just temporary gratification. The first sale is great, but you need continuous sales to be successful.

If you are in it for the long haul, we are committed to teaching you the formula to creating a successful business while you are still working so you can quit your job the smart way and build a successful business at the same time, so you can have everything you want and more.

HOW TO USE THIS BOOK

Real talk, I wish I had this book when I was planning my escape. It would have made my life so much easier to simply follow the format and do what I was told, instead of making all the mistakes I did. But the mistakes were necessary, because out of the mistakes we made came our formula for success. So now we are giving you our system so you don't have to make the mistakes we made and accelerate your escape quicker.

So here's how it works: Inside this book are 6 strategies and recommended escape plan exercises to put our words to work with your action. Read these chapters at least 3 times and do the exercises (we mean it, do the exercises) so you can get your plan out of your head and onto paper.

Listen.

You invested in this book for a reason. Do not let it accumulate dust on your bookshelf or your virtual kindle store. If you are serious about building a business you love, that makes you juicy money every single day, read the entire book and do the exercises, even if it makes you feel uncomfortable.

Here's what we know:

It's easier than you think to quit your job and make money doing what you love

- You don't need to be an expert in your field
- You don't need to have thousands of dollars saved to get started
- You don't have to have it all figured out before you quit

All you need is a passion along with our step by step Escape Plan Formula to show you how to monetize it!

It doesn't matter if you:

- Are tired of working a 9 to 5 where you have to beg for your 2% raise that still can't put gas in your car and leaves you feeling unfulfilled, overwork and underpaid
- A mom (or dad) who hates that you're away from your children 11 hours a day, and are missing out on precious moments you can't get back

- Feel like you are suffocating because you have to hide the real you and put your dreams on a permanent hold, while you are busy getting a lousy check to help someone else make millions.

We are giving you the blueprint, all you gotta do is implement it. It's your responsibility to change your current circumstances.

Now to help you breeze through all the exercises in this book, go ahead and download your FREE Escape Plan workbook here: www.quityour9to5academy.com/escapeplanhelp

Just imagine, Damian and I sitting right next to you, personally coaching you through this process to help you get clarity on every single step in the formula and telling you how to build your six-figure brand. Grab your escape plan workbook now before you start the book.

Get it here =>
www.quityour9to5academy.com/escapeplanhelp

Also, for extra brownie points, make sure to take a picture of your new book and post it on Instagram! Make sure you tag us for a chance to be featured on our website! (@quityour9to5academy) and use hashtag #escapeplanbook

Ok! Now that that's done, let's get started!

#1:
Eliminate Your Fears

"Scared money don't make no money" – Meek Mill

Have you ever stalked Instagram or some other platform and wondered why some people have such huge success over others, namely you?

Have ever felt like everyone else just seems to be killing it in their industry, but you dejectedly watch from the sidelines feeling like life is passing you by?

Have you ever watched someone who was successful and thought to yourself, "I could never do that," or, "I could never be like her or him," "I could never make 6 figures in my business"?

It's ok, if you have. We have to. That is until we decided to stop being spectators to our own life story, and putting ourselves on the court of our lives.

Doubt kills more dreams than fear ever will.

We are usually so busy criticizing ourselves rather than celebrating the accomplishments we have made, whether they are big or small. Confidence comes from a place of self-love, so start loving yourself and celebrating you and your accomplishments!

Stop holding yourself back. If you aren't happy, make a change.

One of the very first things you MUST do in order to create a business you love and make more money which will ultimately give you more FREEDOM is to STOP MAKING EXCUSES!

What are you doing with your day?

How do you spend your time?

Many business professionals often say they don't have enough time to devote to their business, but you have the same number of hours in the day as Beyoncé, yet she finds time to be the biggest pop star in the world, record albums, make movies, do a 3 leg tour around the world, be a mommy and a wife, hang with friends, give back to her community, and so forth and so on... So um... You do have the time.

What you don't have is someone to help you prioritize properly so you can get more done in less time and be more efficient, well until you found us of course!

Your Biography Becomes Your Biology

I will repeat this quote again so you can really allow it to sink in – "Your Biography Becomes Your Biology".

So what does that mean? Well, it simply means that you become what you think and say that you are. The thoughts you plant in your mind becomes hard wired subconsciously and you start to act it out on a daily basis hence becoming your "true" reality.

The language that you use on a daily basis is critical on how you currently operate in your life. Your language creates your reality and speaks yourself into existence.

You create a world of impossibility when you use phrases like:

- I would have
- I should have
- Only if I could
- Maybe one day
- That is not realistic
- I am a loser
- I am trying to
- I cannot do that
- Money is the root of all evil
- I wish I could do that
- I just cannot get a break
- My life sucks

This kind of language is dangerous because it starts to shape your current reality and holds your future of possibility hostage.

Conforming to everyday life can block you from living the life you want to live. Today, most working (and non-working individuals) live every day by the mantra "when in Rome, do as the Romans do." This state of being leads people in the direction of being common, and by this I mean subjecting themselves to replicating the lives others are living. Consequently, they do what everyone else is doing which is also the definition of playing it safe in life and being reasonable leading to an average unfulfilled life.

That sucks and pains me to say it but unfortunately, it is the reality for many people.

I am not exposing this truth to belittle you and make you feel small but I am showing you that you can play a bigger game in life and still live powerfully. So no time for a pity party.

The funny thing now is that living an average and reasonable life is hard so why not challenge yourself to play a bigger game and live the life you want to live?

If you create a new language for your mind now, I promise you that it will be the best decision that you have ever made in your life.

Wherever you currently are in your life IS THE SUBTOTAL OF YOUR THOUGHTS along with the story you have created for yourself.

Always remember that you are guided by your subconscious mind and it is your language that speaks your actions or inactions into existence. Stop looking at your current position in life from a good or bad point of view. Remove the morality side of it and just accept your current circumstances for what it is. I promise you that if you own it and embrace it, this will lead you into a world of living the life you want to live.

Your life should never be hard, boring or average. In fact, your life should be adventurous, unreasonable, complete and wholesome. You should never have the feeling of dreading getting out of bed in the morning to go do what you do.

Always remember that YOU are the architect or designer of your life through your mind.

START CREATING YOUR BLUEPRINT AND ALLOW YOUR BUILDER (Your BRAIN) TO

CREATE A MASTERPIECE of Powerful living then ACT IT OUT IMMEDIATELY.

Remember you are the Designer of your life. CREATE IT AND OWN IT.

To sum it up:

1. Understand that you literally become what you think you are. You must control your thoughts because it manifests who you are.

2. Your limitations are self-imposed fictional stories that have been artificially implanted in your brain by your thoughts, environment, associations and your actions that complement it. You must rise above the narrowmindedness, pettiness and be great with no regrets.

3. You must develop the courage to think positively about your circumstances and just accept it as it is.

Remember you are exactly where you are supposed to be at this moment because the universe does not make mistakes.

People spend most of their lives hoping their circumstances will just go away. I do not believe in hope because hoping never changes your circumstances. In fact, hope is associated with someday in the future which never gets done. Instead, I believe in working the things out from what you say and playing "on the court" of your life, instead of sitting in the stands, by taking the necessary actions to change those circumstances.

So here's how you get rid of any negative thinking you have:

1. Monitor Your Thoughts Daily

You must start to be cognizant of how you are thinking on a daily basis. So start asking yourself, *"How am I thinking on a daily basis? Am I thinking more negatively or positively throughout the day and what impact does this thought process have on my life?"*

2. Build a Foundation of Positivity

You do this by changing your current language that strips you of your power, freedom and self-expression by replacing "I could have", "I cannot", "it is impossible", "I'm trying", and "I should have" – to declarative language like "I AM BEING", "DOING", and "CREATING".

3. Schedule your Positivity Daily

You schedule your positive thoughts daily by writing them down in advance on an oversize calendar, sticky notes, mobile device, or your cell phone. Then what you do is at different times of the day, recite them in the morning when you wake up, at lunch time, and when you go to bed so you can go to bed thinking positively. Also bear in mind that it takes 21 days for this to become habitual or second nature to you so stay consistent. The point of this exercise is for you to develop that muscle memory for you to become habitually positive no matter what is happening in your life.

If you do not schedule positive thoughts in your life, the negative thoughts you have manifested will fill in all the gaps.

4. Honor Your Word of Being Positive

Scheduling positive affirmations in the universe is only half the battle. In fact, your word must be in direct alignment with your actions.

For example, if your job requires you to be in at 9 am sharp and you get there at 9:01am, then you have not honored your word to getting to work on time, even if you don't really want to be there. Mainly because your actions do not correlate with your initial agreement of being on time.

At the end of the day, all we have is our word. Your word anchors you. In reality, people are not designed to honor their word. So when you do not honor your word, do not come down too hard on yourself instead just accept it, move on and create a new action in place that is in alignment to honoring your word.

5. Holding Yourself Accountable

Being accountable to your word is so pivotal because you must hold yourself to a higher standard of completion. If you are not reliable enough to hold yourself accountable, then you must get an accountability partner to hold you responsible for honoring your word.

Accountability creates responsibility.

Remember that language is the source of your transformation. When you have access to a new language, you are open to new possibilities.

Now let's talk about the most powerful two letter word – NO.

Are you afraid of rejection or when someone tells you NO?

I know I was terrified of these two words so much that I ran from my true purpose in life for 38 long years.

Rejection is just a fabricated story people create for themselves. However, the problem is that people make it occur to them as if it is real. Think about the word rejection from this perspective; No one ever says "I reject you."

You get my point?

Rejection and being told no is merely a form of feedback.

Understand that it is part of the journey and not the final destination for your life.

The reason why most people do not reach their destination of living powerfully is because they get off the exit of rejection and the voice in their heads prevent them from getting back on the road of possibility.

Along my journey of life, I have gotten off this exit several times.

You will get off on pit stops in your life during the journey to living your life powerfully, but you must get back on the destination to living the life you want to live.

Running from rejection is a way of being for most people. It is not about being rejected in your life, it is more about the meaning and power people give to the word rejection.

People who live powerfully, aka Entrepreneurs, get "rejected" all the time, accept it, and move on to the next opportunity without recourse because their desire to live the life they want to live burns deeper than their willingness to give up and settle for the life they currently have.

Restore your relationship with the word rejection and you will live powerfully.

This is how you can deal with rejection in two simple but powerful steps:

1. Use rejection as redirection for new possibilities

and

2. Recognize a "NO," as a NEW OPPORTUNITY.

Ok, so now that you got your mind right, let's talk business. Next, we are going to discuss how to create the perfect blueprint your business (aka your escape plan!).

#2:
Strategize Your Killer Business Plan

"If you don't build your dream, someone will hire you to build theirs." – Tony A. Gaskins

So first let us start by telling you this - Never go into business for the money.

If you are leaving your job to create a business you are not passionate about just for the money, you will regret it. If your business is only money driven, it will leave you burnt out, miserable and broke (the opposite of what you are trying to achieve).

People can feel when your heart isn't truly in it and you will be perceived as a sneaky hustler that can't be trusted, who's just in it for the money.

Why waste your time and energy on something you are not passionate about? Trust me, it will eventually rear its ugly head in the end.

So create a business around something you are truly passionate about. It should be something you would never get tired of doing, you love it so much you would do it for free. You feel like you are the best version of yourself while you are in this zone.

So sit down with yourself and really figure out what you are passionate about?

So what I am about to tell you is not about writing your SWOT analysis and figuring out who your competitors are. Oh you thought that's what this chapter was going to be about?

Nope. Sorry.

While those things are super important and you definitely must do that, that's not what this chapter is about. We'll talk about the money a little later. This chapter is about creating the overall vision for your business. If you don't set the pathway in which you want your business to flow, in other words, if you don't know where you are going how can you create the path to get there?

"What isn't INTENTIONAL is ACCIDENTAL"

Yes. You can tweet that.

You've probably heard the saying before, "if you fail to plan, you plan to fail". Quitting your job is a big deal. You need to have a solid plan of action that will successfully take you from employee to entrepreneur.

The last thing you want to do is quit your job without a plan (like Damian aka The Cold-Turkey Quitter) because guess what?

All you're doing is setting yourself up to have to go back into the workforce and conform to getting another job you hate living someone else's dream.

Start getting things in order, think about when you want to quit your job and what that will look like for you.

Start plotting how you intend to make money in your business.

What will you offer? How much will it be? How much money do you want to make monthly? Annually? Who will be your dream clients? Where do they hang out in droves? How will you market to them? How many products or services will you offer? How will you deliver these products or services?

Get a notebook and call it "When I Quit" and start writing your ideas down in this book.

You can try to navigate this process on your own and waste a lot of time and money, or you can find people who have done this before and let them help you. It's your choice.

One thing we do know is that you are already pressed for time. You are working a full-time job AND trying to run a business at the same time hence serving two masters.

Why waste more time and money spinning your wheels trying to figure things out on your own when you can go to an expert who can hold your hand through this process. (And by expert I mean Damian and I).

Invest in yourself while you have a consistent income. Use your job as an angel investor and get with a business coach or mentor that is dedicated to helping you along your journey to both quit and create a successful business.

So it's time to start living with intention. And the first order of business –

SET A DATE WHEN YOU WILL QUIT.

Stop saying, "I want to quit in 2 years, or in 6 months", and set a concrete date. I know it's scary but it works. Beyoncé told you to put a ring on it, and I am telling you to put a date on it. If you don't put a date on it, it means absolutely nothing. So make it concrete and choose a realistic but slightly uncomfortable date. (So don't choose May 3, 2025, but something in the near foreseeable future.)   In March 2015, I made the decision that September 15th, 2015 was the day I was going to quit. I wrote the date down (inconspicuously of course) on a post-it note and stuck it on my monitor, so I would see it every single day I came to work. "091515" is what I looked at every day. Only I knew what it meant, but it was the motivator for me.

Next step:

WRITE THE RESIGNATION LETTER

If it's not written down, it doesn't exist. On March 15th, I wrote my resignation letter and dated it September 15th and even included the 2-week future date that would have been my last date of work. I had already felt a sense of relief after I wrote that letter, it was like I had already quit in my mind, which gave me the battery I needed in my back to push forward with my business.

Now we are going to hold you accountable. Once you've decided on your date, post it in our super private Facebook Group of other Champions like you who are planning their escape too!

You can request access here:
www.quityour9to5academy.com/tribe

Now a word of advice – please don't write this letter and leave it on your desk, or your computer if you have a public space where others can see. We don't want you getting fired, we want you to be in control of when you leave.

If you want to be strategic in planning the best year ever for your business, you have to get crystal clear on who you are, and what your brand means to you, and most importantly why other people should be interested in it.

What is your mission for this year? What do you want to accomplish?

"I want to quit my 9 to 5 and pursue my business full-time on or before May 12, 2017 at 10:00am EST."

What is your overall vision for your business?

"I want my business to be the leading event planning company in my region and I want to have a team of 12 people who manage, plan and design events in Africa, Australia, Canada etc."

How do you want your overall brand to be perceived? How do you want your clients/ customers to feel when they experience your brand?

"I want my brand to perceived as the leading community for hustling entrepreneurs who are ready to leave their jobs to make a difference in the world. I want my clients to feel confident, empowered and ready to take on the world when they experience my brand."

Setting goals and implementing them is the foundation for a successful business. You wouldn't get in a car and travel across the country without your GPS and just ask people along the way how to get to your destination... So why would you do that with your business?

This is your life we are talking about here.

Setting goals helps you create a clear roadmap to where you want to go. There might be bumps or potholes in the road that you have to travel around, there might even be construction which forces you to take a detour, but as long as you have your roadmap the ultimate destination will be the same!

So what actionable goals can you create for yourself in the next 30, 60 and 90 days. Here's a super helpful tip: Get laser focused on what you need to do NEXT instead of focusing on the big picture. When we start thinking big picture, we get overwhelmed, procrastination sets in and we give ourselves an excuse to give up. So think WHAT IS YOUR NEXT STEP. Next steps are more achievable than the "big picture."

Examples of next steps, *"I need a website, I need an assistant, I need to build my email list, I need a business coach,"* ...

Ok, so now that you understand that, it's time to talk about the money...

#3:
Count Your Coins
– How to Financially Prepare to Quit Your Job

"The future belongs to those who plan for it." - Unknown

Most of us are scared to talk about money. Growing up, we have been taught that money is scarce, it doesn't "grow on trees", and it's not free flowing, which is why we can never keep it in our pockets.

Don't blame your parents. Money was probably scarce for them growing up. But we are here to change your thinking and your relationship with and about money. I want you to repeat these words out loud to yourself right now.

Come on, say it with me...

- "Money is *not* scarce."
- "Money *does* grow on trees." (It's paper isn't it?)
- "Money *is* free flowing."
- "Money *is* Abundant in My Life."
- "Money is not the root of all evil."

If you continue to be afraid of money, and don't think you deserve it or can't have a lot of it, you won't. Simple as that. So we need you to recognize, that while it doesn't seem like it now, your money will flow like the Nile River, if you start accepting it into your life.

Now, let's talk about planning to quit. I can probably bet, that 85% of the reason you haven't quit your job yet is because of money. You don't have enough money to feel confident to quit your job, and you've grown dependent on that 15th and 30th check to help you survive.

Makes perfect sense. That's why I stayed at my job for an extra 8 years, because of money. So I get it.

Here's the thing, you have to plan financially to quit. So how do you that? Let us break this down for you.

1. How much are your monthly expenses?

How much money do YOU need on a monthly basis to live the lifestyle you are currently living. Include things like, rent/mortgage, car note, food, clothing, utilities, gas, cell phone, Netflix subscription, cable gym membership, etc....

2. What bills can you get rid of that you can save towards your "Funding My Dream Account"?

For example, like those random trips to the mall, cable TV (everything is live-streamed now by the way), that

Netflix subscription, expensive dinner dates...You will be amazed how much you can save when you start paying yourself first versus splurging on those "feel good items."

3. Determine your Freedom Number

Now, let us explain this for a second. This number we affectionately *call "Your Freedom Number",* is the number or dollar amount you need to make in your business on a monthly basis, that will allow you to be set "free" from the chains of a 9 to 5 job.

So let's say your monthly expenses (including both business and entertainment is $5500). You need to make at least $5500 in your business, on a monthly basis, in order to replace the income you are currently making in your job.

Got it?

4. What product or service can you create now that can help you generate this type of income?

Now don't get all sweaty and anxious on us now. You may not have a product or service yet and that's ok. We are going to show you how to determine this number now, whether you have a product or not.

Business is all about getting paid to do what you love! And in order to get paid you need more clients. Let's get clear on your plan to get new clients now.

What is your monthly revenue goal? And how many clients do you want to work with on a monthly basis? Now, in order to reach the above number of new clients per month, how many new clients would you need to gain each month?

Now let's put it all together to set your monthly financial goal. Take your monthly income goal and divide that number by your monthly client goal.

For example: Let's say you have a coaching business. Your monthly income goal is $5,500 and your Monthly Client goal is 5 new clients each month.

If you want to average $5,500 a month and you only want to work with 5 new clients a month, your average service/product needs to be priced at a minimum of $1,100 to meet your monthly goal.

Now if you already have a program or service that you can market that's perfect. Just make the necessary adjustments to make sure it is priced right for profitability.

If you don't have a product or service yet, ask yourself these two questions:

1. WHAT ARE THE TOP 3 THINGS YOUR CLIENTS WANT FROM YOU? (Think problems they want solved, or desired they want fulfilled)

2. WHAT PRODUCT OR SERVICE CAN YOU CREATE AROUND YOUR GENIUS TO SOLVE THESE 3 PROBLEMS?

Got it? Make sure you download the workbook because we walk you through this exercise in detail so you'll know exactly what to do. (Grab it here = > www.quityour9to5academy.com/escapeplanhelp

Start creating a funding my dream account and call it the "When I Quit" Fund or, "Entrepreneur Fund" or whatever cute positive name you want to call it. Start to stash 3-6 months' worth of expenses in the account.

The one thing you don't want to worry about is how you're going to pay the bills while you're getting your business off the ground. Creating a separate account to fund the production of your dreams will combat that from happening and give you a sense of comfort knowing things will still be taken care of while you're working on your business full-time.

Also, don't commingle your personal funds with funds from your business. You need to keep things separate. This is good for several reasons. For one, it's much easier (and safer) to manage for tax purposes. All your businesses expenses are in one place and can be easily tracked.

The problem I had for a long time, is that when I got paid from a client, I would spend that money like it was a gift. You should always take a percentage of the money you earn to invest back into your business. So it's ok to pay yourself first, but you want to get in the habit of "building wealth" not spending it.

I suggest creating 6 separate accounts, yes I said 6.

1. **Personal**
2. **Savings**
3. **Family**
4. **Household**
5. **Business**
6. **Funding My Dream / When I Quit**

Personal - This is your play money that is used strictly to pamper yourself whenever the heck you feel like it. Nails done, hair done, shoes, basketball tickets, night out with your peeps. That comes from THIS MONEY ONLY. You work hard. So it's ok to treat yourself, just be smart about it!

Savings – This is money you don't touch. You stash it never to be seen again. You'll know when you need to use it.

Family – This is money for family time. So if you have kids, you use this money to go to Chucky Cheese, or the aquarium or the movies, etc. If you are single, then ditch this account and just use the play account.

Household – this is the account you use to pay your monthly expenses – rent/mortgage, utilities, car note, credit cards, student loans, etc.

Business – this account will be used to fund your business. Marketing, Websites, Training, etc. comes from this account.

Funding My Dream / When I Quit – this account is your savings account that is only to be used when you officially quit your day job! These funds can be used to make sure your bills are covered while you are building your dream.

Ideally, whenever you get paid either from your paycheck or from a client, you want to divide your fund by 5 (20%) and put it in each account. So if you made $100, $20 would go into each of the 5 accounts.

Now you can divide the pie however you want, you don't have to divide it equally. You can put 10% in one, and 30% in another and so on, but the idea is to make sure you are putting something in each of these accounts EVERY TIME YOU GET PAID.

This is a game changer for your life.

Ok, next we are going to talk about how to attract more of your ideal clients in droves.

#4:
Attract and Authentically Connect with Your Tribe

"Saying Hello doesn't have a ROI, it's about building relationships." – Gary Vaynerchuk

There is a secret to authentically and effortlessly connecting with your tribe, aka your community, your followers, your fans = the people that will buy from you.

Wanna know the secret? I won't make you wait any longer.

Storytelling.

This generation is all about making connections with people. People don't buy from you because you look good, or you have big muscles, or because you have a PhD. They don't even buy from you because you have the best product on the market.

They buy from you because of how you make them feel.

Statistics show that 87% of purchases are made because of how someone felt. It's the difference between the experience you get at Walmart vs. the experience you get at Target. It's the difference between buying an Android vs. an iPhone (we are team iPhone by the way).

The theory of "if you build it, they will come" is long gone. Now, you have to shuck and jive your way into their hearts if you want to make an impact. Well at least it feels like a shuck and jive if you don't use our formula.

Storytelling is the most effective way to make a connection with your audience.

You have to be relatable if you want to be bankable.

(You can tweet that, just tag us @quityour9to5_)

We wanted to make up something super fancy and mind-blowing for this, but for what?

The formula we use works, except we can't take full credit for it. So, we're going to give you a simple strategy we learned from our mentor and coach, *Lisa Nichols*, to tell your story and steal the hearts (and wallets) of your ideal clients in 2 minutes or less.

It's called The Dip.

The dip is a super easy strategy that will have your ideal clients eating out the palm of your hand. But you have to follow the formula to make this work.

Every good story has 3 parts:

1. Who You Are Now (Here is where you show off all your accolades – and don't be modest either)

2. Your All Time Low (That terrible thing that happened that you don't want anyone to know about)

3. Your Triumph (How you victoriously overcame your struggle and who you have become as a result)

We all have dips in our life...We just choose to keep them hidden. But if you want to be relatable and establish trust and rapport with your audience, you have to meet them where they are and show them that you are human, just like them.

Damian and I shared our dips in the beginning of this book, and I am sure by now you love us, and we feel like family to you. (We love you too and you feel like family to us too by the way!)

That was done strategically. We wanted you to be able to make an instant connection with us from the start. We wanted you to know why we are qualified to write this book and share our success formula with you. And THAT'S what you want to do with your audience.

So here is an example of a dip:

Rhonda is a Certified Life Coach. She is an International Best-Selling Author, with 7 NY Times Best Selling Books. Rhonda has been featured in Essence Magazine, Black Enterprise and was voted Woman of the Year 2017 by Forbes Magazine. Rhonda has a 7 figure coaching practice with over 1.3 million daily followers. But Rhonda's life wasn't always like that.

You see Rhonda often thinks back to the time when she was sleeping in her car, with her 6-month old son, looking for a place to go because her son's father would beat her to a bloody pulp almost every night after coming home from a drunken stupor. This one night he nearly killed her. She waited until he fell asleep and then grabbed her son, and only enough clothes that could fit in her purse and jumped in her car and ran for her life.

She couldn't return back to work for fear he would find her and kill her, so she left everything she knew behind to start her life over. With only $150 in her pocket, she kept driving to get as far away from him as possible, where no one knew who she was. She ended up across the country and lived in shelter for several months before she could get back on her feet. The women's shelter helped her find a job and she started coaching other battered women through their abusive relationships. Rhonda was able to overcome her defeat by empowering other women to stand in their greatness. She's standing tall in front of her attacker and now she spends her life work mentoring and other women to choose themselves and live powerfully.

Now, I just made this up on the fly, so don't go looking for Rhonda or her abusive baby father.

Aren't you instantly rooting for Rhonda to succeed? Don't you want to do anything you can to help her?

That's what storytelling does. It instantly magnetizes your audience to you.

So think now to your life. Who is the "big you" now, and what is something that has happened to you, and how did you overcome it?"

Once you have your "dip" down, you need to master how to tell it in 2 minutes or less.

Why? Because the average person will start to check out after 90 seconds. You have approximately 90 seconds before someone says YES or NO to you.

You have several dips but just use the one that relates more to your audience.

If you are still stuck with what your dip is, here are some questions that you will help pull it out:

Why did you start your business?

What life changing event happened to you?

Did something dramatic happen in your life when you were younger, or even recently?

Did you lose your job?

Did someone important to you pass away?

You don't have to share what you don't want. It's your story, so you tell it how you want to tell it, just make sure its authentic and make sure it resonates with the people who are listening to it.

Don't make anything up. It should be something real to you no matter how big or small you think it is, it will resonate with the right people. Don't use a story that you have not healed from yet.

So now where do you use all this information?

You can use it on your website on your About page.

You can use it when you meet new prospective clients that ask you how you got started.

If you are speaking to large audience at once, (speaking engagements, webinar trainings, etc.)

And of course, you can also share your story on your social media platforms.

So get used to talking about you.

For some of us it's easy to do, we can't stop talking about ourselves, but for most of us, it's hard to talk about ourselves, especially the negatives. If you want some practice, share your story in our super private community on Facebook, where no one will judge you but support you! Just go to: www.quityour9to5academy.com/tribe and request access to join.

Now let's talk about how to package all this up to build get more ideal clients. We share the secret sauce in formula # 5.

5:
Package Your Genius to Create a Magnetic Brand that Steals the Hearts of Your Clients

"Be so good they can't ignore you." – Steve Martin

Let's talk about this infamous word - Branding.

Branding is the topic of year. Before we dive into this chapter, I think it's important to define what BRANDING really is because a lot of people throw that word around loosely and get Branding and Marketing confused.

Here is a simple definition of what marketing and branding really means...

Marketing is: What YOU say about your business.

Branding is: What OTHER PEOPLE say about your business.

Period.

The reason why so many people have difficulty with branding and marketing their business is because what they say about their brand (marketing) and how people perceive their brand (branding) are often conveyed as two totally different things.

It causes confusion amongst your audience, and when people are confused, they don't take action, which means in your case, they don't buy your product or service.

You want your marketing message and the perception of your brand to be in-sync with each other.

For example, if you're promoting a luxury, high-end brand, yet your brand visually screams low budget, it gives the perception of being inauthentic. If your brand doesn't appear authentic, your audience may interpret that as being dishonest or not trustworthy and clients will avoid it like the plague and move on to the next best thing.

It's ok. It's not really your fault.

We have been raised to believe we have to act or look a "certain way" and when we see others doing great things, we tend to copy (ok get inspired by) what they are doing and we start to lose ourselves.

When you try to develop a brand that is not unique or authentic to who you truly are, eventually, the threads will unravel and your clients will see that what you say about your brand doesn't quite match how they perceive your brand.

Mainly because it will be hard for you to keep up this non-authentic version of yourself and the person or lifestyle you may be pretending to be or your messaging doesn't match with the actual experience your clients get.

While you don't have full control over how your brand is perceived by someone else, you do have control over what you put out in the atmosphere in making sure your brand messaging represents your core values and beliefs, so there is no room for error or misguided thinking about who you really are.

The key to having a magnetic brand is to infuse your personality and brilliant qualities into your brand and make your clients fall in love with YOU.

The other part is having a clear and consistent strategy for your brand so that you are authentically you 100% of the time and it is conveyed in your website, your logo, your sales copy, your products and services and the overall experience you deliver to your clients.

Now remember we talked about passion in Chapter 2?

You can be passionate about what you do, but if no one receives the benefit from it you won't be able to make any money. So what problem do you solve for your clients? Why would they be looking for your product or service?

So how do you actually make money doing what you love?

Develop your Sweet Spot

Your sweet spot (in business) is that special place where what you are passionate about offering combines with what your dream clients are looking to buy from you. It's that thing that makes both you and your client giddy when you find each other.

Your signature offer, or what you want to be known for is the offer that completely defines your brand.

This is the best product or service that truly encompasses what your brand represents. So it's very important to get crystal clear on who your dream client is.

It doesn't matter if it's a $5,000 coaching program or a $15 t-shirt. All they want to know is: WHAT'S IN IT FOR THEM?

What can you offer your clients that truly defines what you love to do and is something your dream client would love to receive from you?

Do you know Sarah Blakely, founder of Spanx ™? She is the youngest self-made female billionaire in the world. Sarah invented footless body shaping pantyhose because she was frustrated with having nothing to wear under a pair of tight fitting cream pants and figured if she was having this problem, surely other women were too.

She sold fax machines as her 9-5 job, but hustled her butt off on nights and weekends before she eventually felt comfortable enough to quit her day job and focus on Spanx ™ full time.

Sometimes we over think our business ideas because we have to blow everyone's mind with this innovative product. But Sarah is living proof that it doesn't have to be that complicated.

Is there an unmet need in your market that aligns with your passion that is just waiting for you to dominate it?

Will people see the value and actually use what you have to offer?

Remember your business needs to solve a distinct problem that YOUR IDEAL CLIENTS have. So this is why it is detrimental that you know who your ideal clients are.

Now this is important so listen up... The problem has to be a problem he or she can't live with because it won't move her enough to take action and buy from you.

For example:

Have you ever had a bad toothache?

It starts off as this annoying little pain.

It rears its ugly head every now and then, but it's not life threatening, so you live with it.

Then overtime, if it's not addressed, it becomes this excruciating pain that makes you want to rip your mouth out and feed it to a pack of wolves. (Can you tell I've had one of these before?) You drop everything because you can't take it anymore, and scurry your butt into the dentist to solve the problem for you ASAP!

That's the kinda pain your potential client needs to be in (not physically, of course, unless your product or service solves that problem!)

It has to be something that your ideal client needs an immediate solution to.

Now let's talk about your Marketing.

In order to make all your marketing efforts work like magic, you have to focus on ONE person.

I know, I know. It's a lot to swallow, but let me put it to you this way.

You don't want to spend time talking and marketing to people who will NEVER buy from you. Secondly, when you know the needs of your ideal clients, you know what motivates them to buy from you, which you can now use in your imagery and the language you use.

Need an example?

Ok, let's just say a special somebody that you were interested in was trying to date you.

Would you be impressed if he only had eyes for you, and focused all his attention on telling you how much he couldn't live without you...

OR... would you prefer if he was a straight pimp with 20 other women on speed dial and only wanted an "open relationship?"

Which one would you want to date?

Obviously our prince charming is exhibit A.

Nobody wants to be treated like a number.

You must get into the habit of knowing your dream client so well that you could finish their sentences for them.

When you know your client that well, you can easily craft products and services that they not only need, but values and wants.

You know exactly what flavored ice-cream they need when they are depressed, you could spend hours together gossiping about everything.

I know the idea is a little scary because we are so stuck on not wanting to turn other people off and we want to be liked by everybody.

Would you want 50,000 people who "follow" you on social media but don't buy a thing, or 5000 people who love and adore you and buy your product and services?

Work smarter than harder.

You want to make sure you are talking directly to your dream client, as if they hear you calling their name every time you speak (or market) to them. Knowing this will help you:

   A. Craft services and products that are unique to what they need

   B. Speak their language so that they can identify with you and what you're offering

   C. Allow them to feel special, like your product or service was created just for them

Here's another example:

Think of yourself in a crowded room with a bunch of other men. If someone says out loud, "Hey Guy," then most likely all the men in the room would turn around and wonder, "Who is this crazy person talking to?"

But if the same person says out loud to the group, "Hey Damian," then I know they are talking DIRECTLY to me and now my ears are peaked to pay special attention.

That's how you want your marketing to affect your dream clients.

Sometimes we get lost in the thought that we don't want to niche or target a specific person because we don't want to leave anyone out.

But the truth of the matter is, if you try to target everyone, you end up targeting no one.

You will attract everything BUT dream clients - mostly price shoppers and people who want something for nothing. You will find yourself overworked and underpaid.

That's way more fulfilling than just working to get a check. If you've ever worked a day job, you know that gets tired after a while.

On the other hand, if you approach your business with passion and purpose, your dream clients will naturally be drawn to you.

Your business will be fun and each day will be like a new adventure.

You'll spend your time working with people you love instead of wasting time with people who drain the life out of you.

Remember Niches create Riches.

The other extremely component to creating a magnetic brand is YOU. We spend so much time trying to be like everyone else that we forget we are. If you want to stand out from everyone else doing the same thing, how you can you infuse your personality and guilty pleasures into your business? Those are the perfect ingredients to creating a magnetic brand.

You are not for everyone.

Say it again, but with me this time: "I AM NOT FOR EVERYONE".

Be You. Everyone else is taken.

So how do you actually grow your tribe?

I would be lying if I didn't tell you that there are several ways to grow your tribe, but we'll focus on the most important one – LIST BUILDING.

You must build a list of interested "leads", aka people, if you want to grow your business and eventually grow your bank account. This list of people, are people who have already shown that they are interested in something you have, because they have signed up, or "opted" into an offer (usually free) on your website or social media. Now, when you have new products or services you want to sell, you already have a list of interested buyers!

You can't rely on social media platforms like Facebook and Instagram to build your tribe. Yes, you may have a following on these platforms which is great, but the reality is only 1-3% of those people will actually buy from you. And to add insult to injury, you do not have full control over those platforms. They can change or even shut your account down whenever they want to. Remember when Facebook changed their algorithm and now instead of all your friends seeing your content, Facebook chose who they wanted to show your stuff too? Yeah, everybody got hit when that happened.

Having a list puts you back in the driver seat to share what you want to an email address, not a social media account.

News Flash: You will rarely see people buy from you on their first online encounter with you. They have to be "convinced" that you deserve their hard earned cold cash. Having a lead magnet system really helps to combat this issue because you can deliver delicious useful content to your dream client on a regular basis, which will establish trust.

We don't buy from people we don't trust. Would you buy a Louis Vuitton bag from some random man in a back alley for $25? (Ok, maybe you would... No judgment).

But I'm pretty sure you wouldn't trust the same man to plan your wedding, or style your wardrobe? The same applies to your customers. They have to feel they know you and can trust you with their innermost feelings, which is why creating an email funnel system is so important.

So how do you solve this?

You've got to give her/him something for free to get them hooked. This is referred to as "Your Free Offer, Lead Magnet, or Opt-In Offer".

What that basically means is that you have a sign-up box on your website where you give away a free (book, list, class, video, etc.) in exchange for someone's name and email address.

This person is now called a Lead. They have voluntarily expressed interest in you and your services. The "magnet" is what draws them in.

This will allow you to nurture quality leads that have already shown interest in you and allow you to establish yourself as an expert (aka establish trust!)

If you don't have one already, you need to create a free offer that you can invite your website visitors to sign up for.

Some ideas could be:

    a. An interactive personality quiz

    b. Share a tutorial on how to do something

    c. Share tips, tricks, secrets

    d. Create an eBook filled with great information or resources they can use

    e. A countdown list (Top 5...) People love these!

Offer something that can be of immediate value to them. Think of things you quickly signed up to receive... I'm sure it was free and sure you felt you were going to get some immediate knowledge, know-how, inside scoop from it. Otherwise, you probably would not have signed up for it.

So I know your next question is, "well if I give something away for free, why would they want to buy anything from me? "

(Yeah we can read minds, you didn't know?)

So here is the short answer - You have to share a piece of your expertise with people in order for them to buy into what you're selling. That's just the way it is now. (Blame the internet).

There are a million people chanting the same thing as you to your ideal client, so if you can eliminate an immediate pain for her, you've instantly made a connection.

So what should you give away for free vs. what you should charge for?

Let's keep it real, mostly anything you want to know can be found on the internet. So, you can simple package "The What" into your free offer. What they pay for is your expertise, "The Why."

Think about what information you can share with your audience that they would be grateful to know.

So for example a good example of a free offer is: "3 Things You Need to Automate Your Email List" and a paid offer would be: "How to Set-Up Your Email Funnel Campaign to Generate More Leads".

Got it?

Don't worry, you can practice in the Escape plan workbook. We also list the system we sue for our list building / email campaign systems that you can easily integrate into your website. Just go to the resources page in the workbook.

www.quityour9to5academy.com/escapeplanhelp

6:
Expand Your Network, and Build Your Squad

"Teamwork makes the dream work." - unknown

Most likely, you are a "solo-preneur" which means you are a one woman or one-man show. You are doing it all in your business (you are the CEO, the administrative assistant, the lawyer, the graphic designer, the receptionist, the technician, the accountant, the marketer, the salesperson the web designer and so on.

We don't want you to be a solopreneur anymore.

Now, we understand that in the beginning almost all of us had to boot-strap our business. And that's fine, you start wherever you are, however, you can. But if you want your business to grow and be sustainable, you must take off some of those hats and delegate some of those responsibilities so you can stay in your genius.

This is especially true for all my entrepreneurs out there who are working a 9-to-5 job. I'm guessing you figured out by now that you can't be in two places at once. It doesn't matter how great you've trained your pointer finger to be perfectly positioned with agility and speed on that mouse to minimize the computer screen whenever somebody at work comes around.

You can try to work on your business while you're supposed to be working at your job, but that can take you but so far.

So how do you get things going in your business when you're still working a 9-to-5?

Well, you've got to learn how to both delegate and automate as much as you possibly can. Now before we go any further, I know you're going to say, *"I cannot afford to hire an assistant or somebody to help me."* And that might be true right now but help comes in many different forms, so don't worry, we will show you how you can get help with as little as $5 and in some cases, FREE help!

One thing that I will tell you is, when you do get some coins in your pocket the first thing that you need to do is figure out what you can automate and do it fast because that will save you so much time and money when you're trying to run a business. Because let's face it, who wants to be sitting at a computer screen for 20 hours a day working on their business?

You can do that but you will burn yourself out quick fast. Me personally, I'd like to find a way to work maybe 3 to 4 hours a day on my business and spend the rest of the day doing whatever the heck I please.

Our business has jumped leaps and bounds only AFTER we started hiring help. It was super scary at first, because now I am trusting someone else with my vision baby and, "what if they mess everything up?"

But, you don't see Beyoncé selling tickets to her own show? You didn't see Steve Jobs taking customer service calls for his Macintosh Computers? I certainly didn't see the CEO of The Coca-Cola Company, cooking up the secret formula in the lab.

So you have to let go of some of the control and allow others who are great at what you need help you. We literally record everything we do on our computer or via audio so that we can give that instruction to our team so they can see how we do what we do and follow the same format.

So what should you automate to expand your network?

For starters, you should learn how to automate your list building and email marketing. You need to have an email marketing funnel to help you seed potential clients to buy your products and services without you having to lift a finger.

Creating an email marketing system allows you to bring your clients into your funnel, so once they sign up for your free offer, they'll get a series of emails that will guide them through your process to buy from you.

There are several platforms to do this. We share the platform we use in the Power Workbook.

Digital Marketing. Remember earlier I told you, you can get help for as little as $5? Well, one of my favorite apps of all time is www.fiverr.com. I swear by fiverr.com. If you've got five dollars you can have a whole working office at your disposal. From graphic design, logos, even transcribing.

So for example, here is the behind the scenes of how our blog posts are posted. I record my voice talking, either when I go on my early morning walk every day, or driving in the car, or even doing housework. Then, I send it to somebody on fiverr.com to transcribe and clean it up (because Siri doesn't always understand what I am saying) and then it gets posted on our website.

Simple.

I'm taking one action, which is recording my voice, (I even do this with my Periscopes and Facebook Live videos) and I can pay somebody a few bucks dollars to transcribe that into a blog post. Done.

Definitely worth my time and energy.

Can't afford to pay someone, look for interns in your local universities and colleges.

Delegating also comes in the form of personal help. Like someone who can do laundry for you, or watch your children 2xs a night so you can focus on work, or do light housekeeping.

In the Escape Plan workbook, we share a list of things you can automate and delegate as well as updated links and resources to the platforms we use. We didn't want to list everything in this book, because we want you to have the most recent information at all times, and having this list electronically allows us to update it when needed, without changing the content in this book. So make sure you download it. www.quityour9to5academy.com/escapeplanhelp

Here's a short list of things you can delegate/ and or automate:

Graphic Design

Social Media Posting

Email Funnels

Blog Posting

Dry Cleaning

Housework

There is nothing too big or too small that shouldn't go on this list.

We also outsource a lot of work overseas to workers in the Philippines. I know some of you may be turning up your nose, or scared to give work to someone in another country. But these people are super talented at what they do and because their cost of living is much less than in the states, we are able to outsource more work for less and they appreciate the money they are making for doing what they love to do.

Here Is Your 6 Step Escape Plan Formula

Eliminate Your Fears

Strategize Your Killer Business Plan

Count Your Coins + Prepare Financially To Quit Your Job

Attract and Authentically Connect With Your Audience

Package Your Genius to Create a Magnetic Brand that Steals the Hearts of Your Clients

Expand Your Network and Build Your Squad

Conclusion: So Now What?

So how do you feel?

We have given you our 6 step formula to creating the perfect Escape Plan. Now, this is the blueprint for the Escape Plan. This is not the escape. If you implement the lessons we've taught in this book, and complete the power workbook, you WILL be well on your way to building a sustainable business that continues to grow to the point where you are comfortable to finally hand in that two-week notice.

So what should you do next?

1. Join our tribe of hustling entrepreneurs in our FREE Facebook Group. The group is full of Champions just like you who are working on building their business empire while at their 9 to 5. You will find support, get answers to questions you have from the book or just in your life in general. Plus, we are in the group daily filtering and answering questions. So let's make sure we stay connected! Go to: www.quityour9to5academy.com/tribe to join our tribe now.

2. Follow us on Instagram @QuitYour9to5Academy - there is nothing like getting daily motivation and inspiration while you on your journey.

3. Make sure you check out our other books:

DAMIAN BOOK   TIMEESHA BOOK

There are people out there that are waiting for your genius to brighten their life. Why are you keeping your talents to yourself?

It's time for you to get out there, stop dimming your light down because the people around can't understand you and shine bright like the rare diamond you are!

Use the talents you already possess to create a passion filled, purpose driven life. We've got your back.

Xo,

Damian and Timeesha

MEET THE POWER COUPLE, DAMIAN AND TIMEESHA

Damian and Timeesha Duncan are International Best-Selling Authors and The Founders of The Quit Your 9 to 5 Academy. They rescue gladiators just like you, who want to escape their 9 to 5 to pursue their passion full-time. They will show you how to push through your fears, change your mindset from employee to entrepreneur and gain clarity on building a business of your dreams. Their work has been featured in ABC, NBC, CBS, Fox, The Huffington Post, Upscale Magazine and many other publications.

To learn more about Damian and Timeesha go to: www.QuitYour9to5Academy.com

To book Damian and Timeesha for appearances and speaking engagements please contact hello@quityour9to5academy.com

www.ingramcontent.com/pod-product-compliance
Lightning Source LLC
Chambersburg PA
CBHW070120210526
45170CB00013B/824